Oak Park Public Library

3 1132 01322 6174

OCT - - 2014

OAK PARK PUBLIC LIBR

D1204569

You Can Draw

Trucks

Gareth Stevens
Publishing

Please visit our website, **www.garethstevens.com**.
For a free color catalog of all our high-quality books,
call toll free 1-800-542-2595 or fax 1-877-542-2596.

Library of Congress Cataloging-in-Publication Data

Bergin, Mark, 1961-
Trucks / Mark Bergin.
    pages cm - (You can draw)
Includes index.
ISBN 978-1-4339-7481-6 (pbk.)
ISBN 978-1-4339-7482-3 (6-pack)
ISBN 978-1-4339-7480-9 (library binding)
1. Trucks in art-Juvenile literature. 2. Drawing-
Technique-Juvenile
literature. I. Title.
NC825.T76B475 2012
743'.89629224-dc23

                            2011049302

First Edition

Published in 2013 by
Gareth Stevens Publishing
111 East 14th Street, Suite 349
New York, NY 10003

© 2013 The Salariya Book Company Ltd

Editor: Rob Walker

All rights reserved. No part of this book may be
reproduced in any form without permission from the
publisher, except by reviewer.

Printed in China

CPSIA compliance information: Batch #SS12GS: For further information contact Gareth Stevens,
New York, New York at 1-800-542-2595.

You Can Draw

Trucks

By Mark Bergin

Contents

Introduction

Learning to draw is fun. In this book, a finished drawing will be broken up into stages as a guide to completing your own drawing. However, this is only the beginning. The more you practice, the better you will get. Have fun coming up with cool designs, adding more incredible details, and using new materials to achieve different effects!

This is an example showing how each drawing will be built up in easy stages. New sections of the drawing will be shown in color to make each additional step clear.

1

2

3

4

5

With practice, you too will be able to draw trucks just like the examples shown here.

Materials

There are many different art materials available that you can use to draw and color your vehicles. Try out each one for new and exciting results. The more you practice with them, the better your drawing skills will get!

Use a pencil to draw the shape of your truck. Any mistakes you make can easily be erased, as can any construction lines that are left over at the end of your drawing.

An eraser can be used to rub out any pencil mistakes. It can also be used to create highlights on pencil drawings.

You can go over your finished pencil lines with pen to make the lines bolder. But remember, a pen line is permanent, so you can't erase any mistakes!

Colored pencils come in a huge range of colors and can be layered over each other for new and exciting effects.

Pastels can be smudged and blended together to give you all sorts of different colors.

Felt-tip pens can add vibrant color to your drawing. But remember that they are hard to layer and the color is permanent, so you can't erase any mistakes!

Inspiration

Many types of trucks are made throughout the world. You can choose any of them as the inspiration for your cartoon-style drawing. Looking at photos, magazines, or books can give you new ideas and new designs to try.

When turning your truck into a cartoon-style, two-dimensional drawing, concentrate on the key elements you want to include and the overall shape of the truck.

One way to make your truck look cool is to exaggerate its key features and perhaps add new ones!

Use different colors and designs to make your truck look the way you want it to. It's your creation, after all.

Concrete mixer

A concrete mixer is a specially adapted truck used to transport concrete. The rear container rotates constantly to stop the concrete from setting.

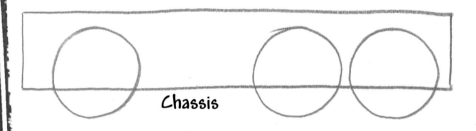

Chassis

Draw three circles for the wheels. Add an overlapping rectangle for the chassis.

Draw in the basic shape of the driver's cab.

Rotating mixer

Add inner circles to the wheels for hubcaps. Draw in the large, rotating mixer.

Draw in the cab window and door. Add the front grill. Draw in the wheel arches and add lines to the rotating mixer.

Wheel arches

Add the driver, side mirror, and door handle. Extend the cab roof at the front and add another circle to each hubcap. Draw in the details at the back of the rotating mixer.

Now add color to the bodywork of your concrete mixer. Complete any final details.

Truck

This truck has a special coupling mechanism that attaches to large trailers so it can haul them over long distances.

Draw three circles for the wheels, with an overlapping rectangle for the chassis.

Add the driver's cab to the front half of the chassis.

Draw in three more circles for the inner wheels. Add the windows.

Draw in the front grill of the cab, then add the bumper and wheel arches. Draw a small circle inside each wheel.

Grill

Exhaust

Coupling

Draw in the driver, side mirror, exhaust pipe, and hubcap. Add the trailer coupling.

Finish your drawing by completing all the remaining details and adding color.

Snowplow

A snowplow has a large blade attached to the front that is used to move huge piles of snow.

Draw three circles for wheels and add a long rectangle for the chassis.

Draw in a large box shape on top of the chassis for the body. Add dividing lines.

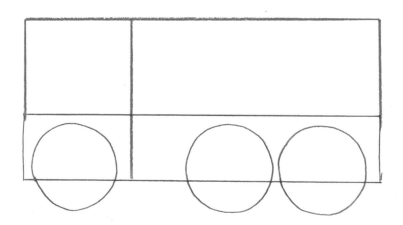

Draw in the window and divide the rear trailer into sections.

Draw in window details and add sections to the trailer. Add two more circles to the wheels for the hubcaps.

Draw the snowplow blade at the front of the vehicle. Add the driver, the exhaust, the wheel arches, and other small details.

To complete your drawing, add snow to the tires and some heaped in front of the blade. Finish all extra details, then add color to your drawing.

Racing truck

Racing trucks are normal trucks that have been stripped down and had their engines tuned up for speed. It's very exciting when these big machines race together.

Draw two circles for the wheels. Add an overlapping rectangle for the chassis.

Add the shape of the driver's cab and the shape of the door.

Add the front bumper, wheel arch, and extra circles for the hubcaps.

Draw in the front grill, window sections, and rear wheel arch. Add two small circles to the wheels.

Draw in the driver and add details to the cab: side mirror, exhaust, and door handle. Draw in the different hubcaps, the trailer coupling, the rear lights, and other small details.

Add color to your racing truck – try making up a racing design of your own! Add any extra details you wish.

19

Monster truck

This crazy truck has huge wheels so it can climb over large objects, even cars!

Start by drawing two large circles with an overlapping rectangle for the chassis.

Draw in the driver's cab. Add two more inner circles.

Roll bar

Draw in the driver's door, the front and rear bumpers, and the roll bar. Add two lines to join the wheels.

Shock absorber

Add the front grill. and the wheel arches (including the giant shock absorbers). Complete the roll bar.

Draw in the driver and add cab details. Add diagonal lines to the shock absorbers. Draw another circle onto each hubcap and add the wheel nuts.

Complete all remaining details, then add mud to the wheels and a cool design on the bodywork. Finish your drawing by coloring it.

Pickup truck

This classic old truck is used to move small loads or even small livestock like sheep!

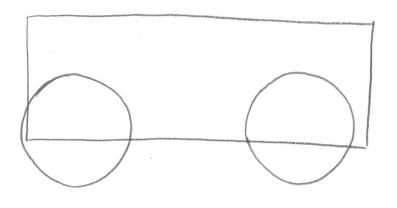

Draw two circles for the wheels and add an overlapping rectangle for the chassis.

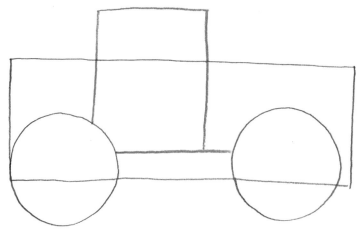

Add a small rectangle for the driver's cab.

Pickup section

Add the roof and the pickup section at the rear. Draw in the front and rear bumpers.

Add in the front grill and draw in the differently shaped wheel arches. Add a window to the cab and circles for hubcaps.

Add the driver, the front headlight, and engine details. Complete the wooden framework at the rear and add the wheel nuts.

Finish off your truck by coloring your drawing and adding any small design details.

Digger

A large bucket with pneumatic arms is attached to the front of a digger. This can scoop out soil from the ground and move it elsewhere.

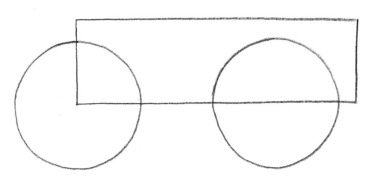

Draw in two circles for the wheels and add a long rectangle that starts halfway through the first circle and overlaps the second.

Add an extension to the rectangle. Draw in the rear shape of the digger.

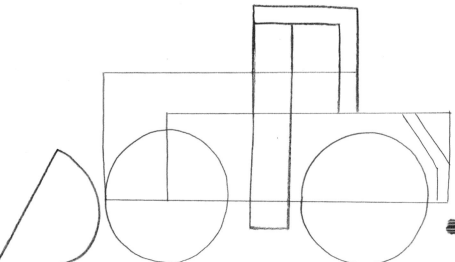

Draw in the shape of the bucket. Add the shape of the driver's cab and steps.

Draw in the complex arm of the digger attached to the bucket. Add two small circles to the centers of the wheels.

Draw in the driver. Add the wheel rims with circles. Add steps and a small exhaust.

Finish off your drawing by completing small details and adding color to each section.

Fire truck

Fire trucks have to carry a lot of equipment, including an extending ladder, but they still need to be fast enough to reach emergencies quickly.

Draw two circles for wheels. Add a large overlapping rectangle.

Draw in the front and rear bumpers. Add the shape of the front of the truck and the detail between the wheels.

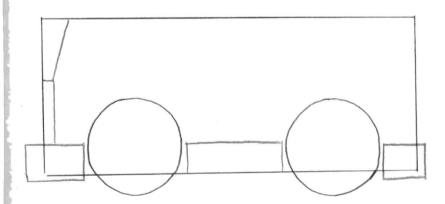

Draw in the wheel arches and two more circles for the hubcaps. Add detail at the rear of the truck.

Using straight lines, draw the ladder on top of the truck and add the detail at the back. Divide the truck body into sections and draw two small circles inside each wheel.

Add a zigzag framework to the ladder. Draw in the windows and add three firemen inside the vehicle. Draw the stripe on the side of the truck and add two different hubcaps.

Complete your drawing by adding all the remaining details and coloring it a bright red!

Earthmover

This giant machine is used for moving vast amounts of earth in open-pit mining operations.

Draw two circles for the wheels and add a rectangle for the chassis of the vehicle.

Copy these shapes to create other sections of the vehicle.

Add more straight lines to extend and complete the main structure.

Mudguard

Draw in the windows and the mudguards, and add two more circles inside each of the wheels. Add a circle for the bumper.

Rail

Draw in the driver and add the rail and ladder. Draw ridges around the edge of each wheel and add wheel nuts.

Your earthmover should be bright yellow. Add a load of earth in the back and brown mud on the wheels.

More views

For an extra challenge, try drawing your trucks from the front or rear! Practicing different views will help you improve your drawing.

Back View

Start with two rectangles for the wheels. Add three horizontal lines.

Draw a rectangle on top and add the cab shape with a curved roof and oval rear window.

Draw in the wooden framework on the back of the truck. Add details underneath.

Add all the little details to finish. A pencil has been used to draw this example. Try other materials to create a different look.

Pickup Truck

Front View

Truck

Start by drawing a rectangle with a line through the center for the wheel arches and bumper. Add two smaller rectangles for wheels.

Draw in the shape of the cab. Add the window and front grill.

Draw in the windows, the front lights, the grill, and the two exhausts.

Finish the front view of the truck by adding these extra details. Then you can color it if you want!

Truck

31

Glossary

bodywork The paintwork on the body of the truck.

cab The part of the truck that the driver sits in.

chassis The frame at the bottom of the main body of a truck.

construction lines Guidelines used in the early stages of a drawing. They are usually erased later.

coupling The part of a truck that links it to its trailer.

exhaust A pipe through which smoke from the engine escapes.

grill A series of slits in the bodywork, near the truck's engine, that allow hot air to escape.

hubcap A metal covering that clips onto the side of a vehicle's wheel.

pneumatic arm A moving mechanism powered by air pressure.

roll bar A safety bar featured in racing vehicles. It protects the driver's head in case of a crash.

shock absorber A device that absorbs the force of sudden, jarring actions.

wheel arches Arches of metal that protect the tops of the wheels.

Index